CW01096237

Addresses & Dreams
(Revised 2004)

To Jan
Love, Best wishes

Paul McC

January 2007

Also by Pauline Prior-Pitt

Waiting Women 1989
(Revised Edition1999)
ISBN 1 872916 29 5

In the Heat of the Moment (1992)
ISBN 1 872916 19 8

Still Standing in the Plant Pot (1994)
ISBN 1 872916 27 9

Storm Biscuits (2001)
ISBN1872916 31 7

Waiting Women CD
A recording of selected poems

PAULINE PRIOR-PITT

ADDRESSES & DREAMS

(Revised Edition)

SPIKE PRESS

ADDRESSES & DREAMS
revised edition
published by SPIKE PRESS in 2004

ADDRESSES & DREAMS
first published in 1997
reprinted   1999

Publisher: SPIKE PRESS
112 Broomfield Road, Coventry CV5 6JZ
Tel: 01876 560360

Distributor: AVANTI BOOKS
8 Parsons Green Road, Stevenage SG1 4QG
Tel: 01438 745876

Printed and bound in Scotland by Highland Printers
13 Henderson Road, Longman North, Inverness IV1 1SP

ISBN 1 872916 32 5

Acknowledgements:

This edition of ADDRESSES & DREAMS includes poems that
first appeared in "Still Standing in the Plant Pot"
Several poems first appeared on BBC Radio 4 and in
THE MAGAZINE
'Making Babies' first appeared in THE INDEPENDENT

Pauline Prior-Pitt is a freelance writer, performer and after dinner speaker. She now lives with her husband on the Isle of North Uist in the Outer Hebrides but travels to the mainland several times a year to give performances and to see her three children and her two grandsons.

Thanks are due to Sally McKeown, editor of SPIKE PRESS, and to William Shaw for their help and advice with this revised edition.

For
Robert
Paul
Charlotte &
Adam

CONTENTS

THE EDGES OF MY MIND

You occupy the edges of my mind
Waiting to be summoned into thoughts
Filling me with longing and with guilt
For all those opportunities ignored.

But life stands on my doorstep every day
Demanding, using, eating up the hours
And years drift into decades, separating.
We lose the bonds that once held us so close.

Oh I would like to stretch my arms out wide
And gather you all to me in this place
To look upon each face in turn and say
How I have missed you all along the way.

Yet every day I summon one or other
And slowly pleasure in that time we had
Knowing that we cannot be together
It's gone and we have changed, there's no return.

And do you think of me sometimes I wonder
Do I occupy the edges of your mind?

STILL STANDING IN THE PLANT POT

You, still standing in the plant pot, answer!
Was the soil warm, securing in the dark your roots
contained? Did you face the pruning courageously,
pared down dutifully to the correct shape,
tied to a stake, trained?

Could you cope with inconstant watering,
almost drowning, your roots bloated with drink,
left for days in parched earth, bitter, drained?
And when you needed shade, did you remain
in your place in the bay window?

About the buds bloodstained in their bearing
did you feel guilty when some didn't bloom?
Tell the truth about the dead leaves
Was it your fault they withered?
Were you ashamed?

Think carefully about the next questions
Did you at any time stare at seagulls?
Did you thirst to go out when it rained?

SIFTING THE LINEN

And when finally they have gone, what then?
Will you come slipping back so easily
to find your remains after the long years
of silence? Princess Aurora sleeping
for a hundred years was still sixteen.

Your marks are here like bruises after battle.
Sifting the linen, you lift down sheets,
open them, fold them and refold them
in their old creases, search for holes
worn in pillowcases, where there are none.

You dredge your fingers along ledges
disturbing no dust. In spare rooms, beds,
made up just in case, bear no trace
of messy adolescence. The surfaces you polish
already gleam and every drawer reveals

folded neatness. Enter each room.
Your marks are here like tracings on paper
the original fast fading, just remaining.
Will you sit on here, cosily slipping into Grandma,
or will Aurora wake you with a kiss?

ON THE BRINK

Just by chance, she sat
at the next table. Radiant.
Not a trace of the jaded nurse in her.

Had she found another man?
I must be crazy to think
of such constraints, she said.

She was painting again,
hadn't touched a brush in years,
blamed the landscape of her marriage,

the lack of space. Thought
something about the brink of being fifty
had given her permission.

AT FIFTY

That is how it was for her
always sailing out
where wind against tide
lifted off wave tops.

At the helm, heading her prow
into breaking seas
sail reefed, a white triangle
against the flood.

In harbour calm,
away from the wind, the woman
who has stopped bleeding
kneels beside a small canoe.

WITHOUT DISTURBING THE RIVER

When she heard the man on Radio 4 say
"In the middle of every onion is a tear",
she wrote it in her note book,

carried it everywhere like treasure,
the tight layers of silent flesh holding it in,
the papery skin, how breaking into it with fingers

would be difficult. Easy with a knife.
Reckless. Slicing straight down
but she was afraid they would all drown.

Safer to crouch under the waterfall,
where sobbing would not be heard, where
tears could spill without disturbing the river.

IF I HAD KNOWN THAT SHE WOULD CALL

If I had known that she would call
here for coffee at half past ten,
I would have cleaned the house, and then
made a delicious chocolate cake
to eat off flowered patterned plates,
ground coffee served in matching cups.

But I am glad I didn't know.
She came, she saw, there was no show;
the dusty mess the house was in,
the sink of pots, the floor of crumbs
the ginger biscuits from the tin,
the instant coffee out of mugs.

She hadn't come to see my house.
She held me close and kissed my lips,
didn't mind the untidiness.
We sat entranced, in company.
She'd come to share her soul with me.
We spoke of love and poetry.

COMPANY OF WOMEN

Something comforts
in the company of women,
earthed in the sharing
of our mothers.

Daughters born in pain
to bear again the cycles
of the moon's swell
of tidal water at the flood

the shed of blood, motherhood.
Forever bound in the guilt
of not being good enough
but wanting more.

We give permission
unroll each other's grief,
soften the pain,
hold the broken bone.

THE GLASS CEILING

She walked the cliff path
in the shelter of trees
the winter sun on her back
lulling her to summer.

She did not see
cloud on dark cloud
gathering to overtake the sun and her
soon to drench
blaming with hail
for trusting in such pale sunshine.

She sat in her office
sheltered by the young man's solicitous smile,
before he gathered her brainchild into his cloud
and overtaking like the storm strode on.

Leaving her stranded on the cliff.

Such an ancient cliff.
Erosion cracks concealed in the grass
poised to plunge into the sea.

ON HER OWN

She's on her own, at home alone.
There's no one near to interfere.
No one to say will we be having lunch today.

She's not on call. No one at all
is there to interrupt her mood,
to spoil her quiet solitude,
asking where his trainers are
and will she be needing the car.

She's on her own, completely alone
doing what she wants to do
not what others want her to
enjoying every single minute.
Wouldn't ever dare admit it.

THE MAMMOGRAM

They squeeze your breasts.
Oh I said
Hands cupping mine in bed.

They spread your breasts onto a plate.
Oh I said
Spreading pâté on bread.

The X Ray comes down and presses you hard.
Oh I said
Smoothing sheets on the ironing board.

They squash your breasts until they're flat.
Oh I said
I don't fancy that.

You want to scream and you think you'll burst.
Oh I said
This gets worse.

The edge of the plate digs into your side.
Oh I said
And I felt afraid.

It's called a mammography machine.
Oh I said
Designed by a man? It must have been.

OFF GUARD

Beyond the cave, sand
soft as breasts to sink in, he said
as they staggered
hand in hand
to the sea. Not
quite believing it.
Together in water
Floating at last.

They were off guard,
careless of the toppling wave
coming out of nowhere,
surging them
to the back of the cave
to the smashed bottles
and the shivering.

MY FATHER, THE ACCOUNTANT

And yet to account had been his life
Accounting at work, accounting at home.
Constantly asking, "Are you all right?"

Checking we had our fair share.
Each experience carefully weighed.
Anxiously adding the pros and cons.

Subtracting danger, filing our fears.
Correcting events. Protecting us all
from real life. Unbalancing our view.

So when he said in old age,
"Life has gone so quickly, I might as well
have been a tramp"

it shocked us all. It was as if
all he stood for was of no account
and yet to account had been his life.

FEELING THE COLD

He should never have worn slippers in the first place,
always wore shoes indoors, brogues with laces.

These were the kind he'd scorned for years,
laughed out loud at them in shop windows.

Now he thought the sheep's wool lining
would be cosy, grey plaid not too showy

drawing my attention to the way the whole foot
was covered, like slipper boots

and the convenient Velcro fastening
saved bending down.

What shift of thought rejected shoes, sought
comfort in slippers to shuffle round the house.

He had his reasons. Windows flung open every morning
for through drafts, stayed shut.

He wore a cardigan over his jumper.
Said he was preparing for a hard winter.

CHRISTMAS ALONE

Waking without the wrapping paper crackle
when she piled his presents onto their bed
and nestled up for a Christmas waking kiss.

Drinking a mug of lonely morning tea. Thinking
of the Christmas mountain he must face today.
No need to hurry down to play
`Christians Awake' on her piano.

Trying to smile in church.
Breaking down on favourite carols.
He cannot pray.

Taking whisky to his brother's.
The fuss they make of him,
piling turkey with the trimmings on his plate.
She would have put more salt on it he thinks
and shakes more on.

Staring at tinsel in the fairy lights.
Winning at cards.
Leaving early
before they play charades.

FINAL FLING

It was as if his old bones
had known about this day,
got him up early to face it,
scrapping his usual routine

of staying in bed,
too confused on his own
to know what to do,

waiting for the one familiar face,
mine, to help him dress,
even then calling me Martha,
naming his loss.

Cold in pyjamas, he stood
like an ancient sower,
flinging mauve tissues from a box
decorating his room
as if in celebration.

THE SCATTERING

One leading,
one so pregnant it was dangerous,
one holding the box
slid down the cliff grass, searching.

It could have been a day like this
when he was scattering her ashes.
They didn't know.
                 He chose to be alone
but in March you can be fairly sure
of a strong North Easterly above Hornsea beach.

They didn't know
if this was what he wanted
if this was the same part of the cliff.

If they were expecting comfort from his remains
they were shocked. Nothing looks
so final as that metallic ash.

It spewed from the box. Fled in the wind
towards the shore, covering them,
clinging to their wet faces, staining them grey.

MAKING BABIES

Making babies is
sweet lips gentle
his hands softly
softly exploring,
touching where I
want to be touched
helping me,
helping me to come
inside me his seed,
his smile above.

Making babies is
rough lips forcing
hands holding me down
uniforms sweating,
sweating above
making me,
making me,
making me bear,
making me bear my enemy's child.

They need to extend their bloodline.

BATH TIME

And after the whole exhausting day of it,
she kneels beside the bath
to wash three upturned faces,

feels the soft creases of chubby necks, squeezes
Pears-soaped slippery skin to cleanness,

fills the jug three times, streams clear water,
leaves them clean to splash and slide, spill over.

Soaked and sick tired she sits on the loo, watching,
not seeing them. Wanting something more.

And in the gas chambers they say mothers gripped
their babies' hands that in the stiffening of death

their fingers could not be parted. She lifts them out
one by one to warm towels, wrapping them,

scenting them with Johnson's powder,
drying between each precious toe and finger
with her two hands.

AFTER

Were we ever
together
after
our new
love
slipped
between us
like butter

after
I saw him
finger
your breasts
his sucking
mouth
in place
of mine

after
I lay
in our bed
hearing you
tending
his cries
not hearing
mine

after
you gave
him
the special
smile
I thought
was mine.

SOFT IN HIS COT

In her dream he lies soft in his cot.
There are no cries in her dream.

On his back helpless
Sucking his thumb, one arm flung out.

Cruel fists do not bruise delicate flesh.
No violent hands shake tiny bones to silence.

In her dream he lies soft in his cot.
Pink in her dream.

CLUTTERING CHILDREN

I have seen you shopping,
your cluttering children
whining in the trolley
hiding in the aisles.

Like you I have queued
at the bacon and cheese
wanting to cry, a pound
of mild energy please
and five slices of time.

I do not envy you....
their sleepy bedtime smiles,
their angel cheeks on mine.

JUST

Your mother and I
are just going for a walk
he said to the children
just old enough to be left.

It must have been summer
the willow just arching over the steps
in the early evening
and just enough light after supper.

Just round the block,
we'll soon be back
and we just left them on their own
for the first time.

We just walked out
through our gate
like prisoners just released
looking back, expecting them.

In the park
he pushed the swing
just high enough,
me squealing like a girl.

CRICKET ON THE BEACH

Just here, I say. Here where the sand is washed
by the tide, soft dried in the wind and sun.
Just here, the mothers in cardigans and frocks,
spread the rugs you couldn't sit on if you got too wet,
settled the picnic bags you couldn't touch
and nestled into deckchairs with knitting.

Here, by the breakwater, where the pebbles stop
and the sand flattens down to the sea, just here
we'd meet and all play cricket on the beach.
No teams, each one against the rest. The dads
arranged the order. You had to earn your turn
by fielding first, sometimes splashing into the sea.

That's the 'Marine' where the dads disappeared,
came back smelling of beer. No cider for you, they'd say,
hiding the bottles. We could always find them.
Cider at the seaside, egg sandwiches and potted meat.
Sit down to eat them please. We don't want sand
in the sandwiches. Can it be a sandwich without sand?

Oh yes we'd swim, in the afternoon, not too soon
after the picnic, you might get cramp and drown,
and not out of your depth. When the tide had turned
and the sea crept in over the warm sand.
We wanted waves with curling crests to dive through.

Then the walk along the shore to warm us.
Some of the mothers paddled with the little ones.
He and I walked way ahead searching for shells.
Don't go too far off they'd say, and we
would wave and wander farther off to where
the cliffs begin. And we would sit and kiss.

Then wander back for ice cream and the castle
strong enough to stand against the tide.
Everyone must dig. The little ones cried
losing their spades to dads. They carried buckets
of water up the beach to fill the moat
and stuck their paper flags where they could reach.

We wouldn't leave until the castle perished,
until the sea rose over the pebbles, until
it covered the soft dried sand, until
there wasn't any sand for us to stand on.
But you and I, before the tide comes in,
shall we walk along the shore to where the cliffs begin?

MY CAR

He's passed his test. Can he borrow the car.
I say it's not 'the' car, it's 'my' car and wonder why
mine is the car he's insured to drive.

His Dad's is bigger, newer
more expensive in every way
but only drives from A to B and B to A each day.

Mine is superwoman's chariot
battered car of the daily circus
the juggling can't start without it.

I suppose when I'm not using it.
If he doesn't start abusing it,
showing off, driving too fast just for a laugh.

But before he treats my car as his
I'm writing some rules.
Here is the list:

Never forget it's your mother's car. Drive
as if it belongs to your father
and he's sitting behind.

My car's not yours to drive by right.
It's on my terms. Always be grateful.
Take extra care at night.

Don't promise to drive your friends to the pub
the match, the club, before asking me
if the car will be free.

If I say, 'No' it will be for a reason. Don't try
to make me change my mind. Don't imply
I'm growing senile. Try to be kind.

Remember,
when the little light comes on the car needs fuel.
Leaving it for me to find first thing in the morning
when I'm charging to work, is cruel.

Remove sweet papers, curry cartons, cans of coke.
Don't ever, on any account,
let your smoking friends smoke.

Look in the boot from time to time.
The football boots, trainers, sleeping bag,
sweatshirts, dirty socks, are not mine.

Finally, if I ask you to clean it, don't say
you haven't time, don't say you'll get around to it.
Just do it.

STUDENT

He's home for the holidays,
a term's dirty washing
spilling from his backpack
onto his bedroom floor.
You can't open the door.

Leave it he says.
I'll sort it tomorrow.
And tomorrow and tomorrow
I say. He's out all night
and he sleeps all day.

I try to sort his washing
into piles: colours, woollens, whites.
There are no whites.
There's nothing vaguely bright.

Everything has assumed
a sameness, varied shades
of a dirty greyness.
I wash the lot, the paler greys on hot.

Then hang them on the line
to dry and realise
half of his clothes
I don't recognise.

This isn't his shirt
His towels were green.
There aren't many socks.
Whose knickers are these?

Now they're ironed and folded
neat piles on his bed
He's grateful of course.
He was going to do it.

Somehow he just didn't
get around to it.
Now leave them he says.
I'll put them away

But you know where they'll be
When you open his door.
They'll be back where you found them,
all over his floor.

RED BALLOON
(for Charlotte in New Zealand)

In the middle of my night
you rang with sunshine in your voice
in my ear, near enough to touch.

How strange it felt, knowing
your day was almost over
and fading into autumn, and mine

was still to come with snowdrops.
Like mother and daughter
upside down, caught out by time.

Now in an early morning dream, I hold
in my arms a red balloon, which grows
until it is too big to hold, and I let go.

RAG DOLL

I never played with dolls and nor did she,
her dolls pram filled with mud to yank across
the garden making roads for her brothers' soldiers
and their plastic tanks.

Her rag doll sat forgotten in an odd box,
at the end of a house move, left unpacked.
Her bedraggled state disturbed my maternity
for one whom I had made to be now so neglected.

Her pantaloons, the blue daisy patterned dress,
the lace trimmed smock washed and pressed looked
nearly new. Her hands well scrubbed became
a paler grey. Her cotton face,

her pretty cotton face, wore stains of grief
that would not wash away. She sits
propped on my window sill. Some of the stains
are fading in the sun.

WHO WILL THREAD THE NEEDLE NOW?

In our dream, Grandmother,
you're in the back room
kneeling on newspaper.

I know you're there,
the Brasso's in my nose
when I hang my satchel in the hall.

There's a shilling on the shelf
and treacle toffees
twisted in brown paper .

You hand me a clean duster
for the shining
and the brasses gleam.

You mend the linen for my mother,
little portcullises darned into vests,
hems caught up with tiny stitches.

"Thread the needle for me, bright eyes," you say.
The needle's eye looks huge to me
and I am proud to thread it easily.

You grab it back and stab and stab my cheek
until it bleeds onto a map
spread out below our feet.

You stand by the Humber.
I'm by the Thames in my cap and gown
and never coming back.

Your dead hand spins a globe
above my head, spreading
our blood onto far continents

from where the bright eyes
of my children's children
gaze back at me reproachfully.

"Who will thread your needle now?"
you scream. "Look at your brasses,
they no longer gleam."

LIKE DAISIES IN GRASS

Like daisies in grass, easy
I help paint your kitchen
cream over anaglypta. Not

an experienced decorator, but
I have painted walls before.
I know the strokes. Not

like your new mother,
all those years ago,
with a blank CV in mothering.

You taught me, besotted me.
And our first year was as near heaven
as any. And as we walk

into Earlsdon to buy ham on the bone
and wholemeal rolls, it's easy
like daisies in grass.

SISTERS 1
(for Jean)

A champagne day
driving into town
cool in make-up
smelling of Chanel
sucking our mintoes
shopping for clothes.

We avoid the anorexic
dresses on their hangers.
Something fuller, smocky,
loose. You choose blue,
as always, and for me
dull green in creased linen.

In the café we change
our table three times
getting it right. You
divide the toffee apple cake
into equal pieces. I
pour the tea. We deserve this.

THE DRESS FROM HOBBS

I met you in Cheltenham
pressed between other dresses
bedraggled linen, blue/grey
with sisters in pale navy.

I held you close,
searched my eyes in the mirror
then walked away.

But later on that day,
in curtained privacy,
you slipped over my head,
settled on my breasts,
the rest floating almost to the floor.

You did your best to flatter,
so well cut, deceiving slim,
sleeveless creasing linen.
I did not give in.

In Nottingham
I glimpsed your navy sister.
She did her best but oh the cost.
I loved her, then I left her.

Yesterday I went to Cheltenham again
and called to see if you were waiting,
and you were. I loved you even more.

The creases didn't matter.
We could iron them out.
And damn the cost,
it's not often I'm so flattered.

I brought you home,
bought you beads
of blue, grey, gold and terracotta.

I'm taking you to France,
to sunny weather
for you are going to flatter me
all summer.

BLACK DRESS

In her wardrobe hanging
lonely, separated from the rest,
a black silk slip of a dress
minute beads on finest threads
fanning out like spider's webs.

She danced with nothing on beneath it,
rather shocking, just black stockings.

Her wrinkled hands caress the dress,
the nothing on beneath his body
hard against her bone, the silk thread,
beads of sweat, the black dress
crumpled on the floor.

FITTING

The Spirella lady sipped tea
from our thin china.
The cake stayed on the trolley.
Perfectly still on the settee
I wasn't offered any.

She opened her case.
Shook out tissue-wrapped
biscuit-pink cambric.

And mother stood, shy
without her clothes
in the middle of the afternoon
her crossed arms
dressing her ample flesh
long laced, curvaceous
waisted, stayed.

Round her bottom
chubby suspenders
dangling free on her fat thighs
and over the top
her pinched back spilling
like cream in the cake
when she cut it.

NEW SCARF

Tuesday
afternoon.

Stratford.
Monsoon.

Fluffy bit of stuff
for my neck.

Chenille scraps
in grey and black.

In the Post Office queue
met someone I knew.

"Can I feel
your chenille?"

I said,
"Do!"

AGEING FRAGMENTS

I. SHE

She looked in the mirror.
She stared in alarm.
She climbed the stairs slowly.
She tried to stay calm.
She entered her bathroom.
She locked herself in.
She picked up her tweezers.
It was time to begin.
She plucked a black hair from the side of her chin.

II. OLD NECKS

Old necks are not nice.
Suddenly there's twice the skin
Hanging underneath your chin
And you can't tuck it in.
You could have it cut in half
Or just wear a scarf.

III. OSTEOPOROSIS

You notice your bosom
Which suddenly drops.
You notice your bottom
Which suddenly flops.
But you don't notice
Osteoporosis.

IV. GLASSES

Print is not so big.
Print is not so clear.
I hear my mother's voice in mine.
"Have you seen my glasses dear?"

V. PUBIC HAIR

Why is my pubic hair so dark
And the hair on my head so white?
My white hair is so public.
The pubic's out of sight.

LEVELLED

Do not ask me to play Bingo.
And if we have to be familiar,
my name is Josephine, not Jo
not Flower, not Petal, not your love
and not your 'favourite girl' again today.
No I will not join the sing-song, not play
cards, not learn so late in life to knit.
Just wheel me over to the window
I would prefer to sit here on my own and reminisce.

Other mistresses playing lawn tennis,
chaise longues on the terrace,
iced gin and tonics, quoting from Horace
Shakespeare and Marlowe, the long slow adagio.
Old girls visit me infrequently.
I can, given the opportunity, still speak
"Shall I compare thee to a summer's day" from memory.
Sadly, no one here is impressed.
I might as well save my breath.

VENUS

Her hands can barely lift
the fork. Like an old hen, she
scratches the potato on her plate,

and sides grey meat. It is too tough
for her to cut. The nurses call her
'Flower' as they rush.

And if you look into the sky tonight
says John Ketley on her wireless
you will see Venus, the bright star.

She lifts her head, leaving peelings
in the sink, a meat pie in the oven,
to look into the bright sky.

AMNESIA 1

At the top of the stairs
is the chair where I sit
when I can't remember
what I've come up to get.

I know it's no use sitting there
I'll have to go back to exactly where
I was, when I thought about going to get
whatever it is that I've forgot.

AMNESIA 11

I go upstairs to get my purse
from my bag on the bedroom chair.
I put shirts onto hangers, gather
clothes for a wash and take them downstairs.

I go upstairs to get my purse
from my bag on the bedroom chair.
It's started to rain, the windows are open
those flowers are fading. I take them downstairs.

I go upstairs to get my purse
from my bag on the bedroom chair.

On the bedroom chair is yesterday's paper,
the unfinished crossword, 10 down, 7 letters,
something 'M' something 'E'
and I can't remember the word for loss of memory.

AMNESIA 111

I have to write everything down now
make notes in my diary
then make a note saying,
'look in your diary'.

I make lists, lists of lists
lists saying 'make a list'
daily organising lists:

1. Bank, take out fifty pounds
2. Buy a card for Rose
3. P.O. stamps and post
I forget the list
go straight to the P.O.
don't know what I've come for
go back home.

If I'm just going for one thing
say a Battenburg cake
I don't make a list
but that's a mistake.
I see ripening peaches
fancy a few grapes
wonder if I'm out of bleach
am tempted by the fillet steak.
I leave the shop with a carrier full
but no cake.

I keep pens and paper by my bed
for when I can't sleep.
Last night I scribbled

1. Crackers
but are they for Christmas, for cheese
or is it someone I know?
I don't know.

If ever I find I've written
1. Get up.
I'll give up!

LET ME INTRODUCE

Let me introduce…
My mind's gone blank.
This is ridiculous.

She's been my friend for forty years.
She came to my 8th birthday party for heavens sake.
We sat together at junior school.
We both remember the silence and the smell
when Elaine couldn't wait any longer
and left the room, without leaving.

We cycled to the high school together
for seven years, five miles in a head wind,
refusing to wear sensible knickers.
We both remember the horrible stew we wouldn't eat,
piling it all onto one plate till it brimmed over.
Screwing our faces when the teacher said, "People
in India who were starving would be very grateful."
And we offered to take it.

We slept together in the same bed when lesbian
was a word we'd never heard. We made
all those hearts for the Valentine's Dance.
Tommy Steele was singing the blues
and Elvis made us feel funny 'down there',
but we couldn't explain it.
We should have been bridesmaids
at each other's weddings.

I know her name as well as my own.
It's on the tip of my tongue.
Let me introduce…

ROMANTIC LOVE

I shall not compare thee to a summer's day.
It has been done before and anyway
Thou art not more temperate.
To make a willow cabin at your gate
Would only block the way and cause delay.
How easy for those early poets to write
Of unrequited love that burned so bright.
Their passion lasted for such short a time
No wonder then to think their love sublime.

Romantic love ignores the follow up
Lives happily ever after, doesn't do the washing up.
A love that lasts for over thirty years
Must settle to a passion more serene.
And yet I must confess you still possess
The power to make me feel, just seventeen.

CHECK VIYELLA SHIRTS

"It was his check viyella shirts." I said.
"His dark green duffle coat when everybody else
was wearing camel, his outrageous satin waistcoats.
One was purple shot with lime."

Well that was what I told my vicar, when he said,
"How do you know you love this man?"
This man not being present at the time.

I wasn't going to tell him we'd been lovers
in the days when we were Vikings
setting out from Norseland's ancient shores.
That finding him again was coming home.

I wasn't going to tell him that September smells
are closer in St. James' Park, that leaves set fire
to paths in autumn, that late evening mists the lake,
that we always thought the ducks were watching us.

I wasn't going to let him know about the flat
in Holland Park, with its huge enamel bath.
How he cooked my breakfast every morning.
How the standard lamp kept falling. Every night.

And I wasn't going to say we were in love
with T.S. Eliot. How we searched the streets
of Notting Hill for "muttering sputtering" gas lamps
to feature in our film. And that was how we came
to find the shop that sold the ring.

And after all those days of laughing,
I wasn't going to tell him how his green eyes
looked so solemn, when he asked me if I'd marry,
slid the ring onto my finger. How it was like
looking in a mirror, we were reflected in each other.

How we knew we'd waited centuries for this.

ANSWER PHONE / THREE-TIMING

Hello, this is Joe.
Sorry I'm not at home.
Please speak after the tone.

Hello Joe, it's Fiona.
Just phoning to let you know
I'll be round tonight at eight.
Love love you do, so.

Hello, this is Joe.
Sorry I'm not at home.
Please speak after the tone.

Hi Joe, it's Jan.
Just to say tonight's OK.
If I can
I'll be there at eight.
I can't wait.

Hello, this is Joe.
Sorry I'm not at home.
Please speak after the tone.

Joey. It's Little Me.
Guess what, after all
tonight I'm free. I'll call at eight.
I won't be late.

……………………………

This is Fiona on 74260.
There's nobody here at the moment
Leave a message after the tone.

Fiona. This is Joe.
I didn't know
you were coming round tonight at eight.
I won't be here. I'm working late.

This is 63772.
Sorry I can't speak to you.
It's Jan. I'll get back to you
as soon as ever I possibly can.

It's Joe, Jan.
No Jan.
Don't come tonight.
I won't be home 'til after ten.
I'll try and phone you then.

Hello, this is 26633, Little Me.
Sorry I can't speak.
Please leave a message
after the bleep.

It's Joe, Little Me, Sweety Peety,
so glad your free for Great Big Me.
What a treat. See you tonight at eight.
Don't be late. I can't wait.

....

Hello. This is 26633
Little Me really speaking

Hello. This is Joe really speaking.
Where are you Little Me? I'm waiting.

I know Joe. Sorry it's so late.
I know we've got a date for eight
and now it's nearly nine.
Darling Jan and Fiona are here.
Did you know they were friends of mine?
We've drunk an awful lot of wine…….

Why don't you come over dear
or will Great Big Me see his Sweety Peety
some other time?

Joe, I'm waiting for you to speak…………………

PRIVATE VIEW

Did we come all that way for this?

"Lovely to see you darling! Kiss, Kiss"

There must be something more,
something more than daubs surely,
more than sawdust daubed with ordure.

"Awesome darling"

Not more frames of slit silk representing rape.
Not another ochre mess, a child of five….
Let me guess. Untitled piece. Surprise, surprise.
Ah! A black canvas with one pale pink line
entitled `Clandestine'.

"Daring! Divine!"

Now that's absurd. Read the blurb.
Apparently the big toe stapled to the rat,
exposing bone, is his own.
Grown men should be ashamed.

"Amazing darling!"

Now this has appeal.
The smoked salmon looks almost real,
and the brown bread…

*"Oh! Thank you. Delicious darling.
Sparkling wine. Sublime!"*

Darling, what's the time?

PISCES

Wake me slowly. Let me
float here anchored inside myself,
gently abandoning my dreams
from the rim of sleep. All night
I have swum in deep pools

catching the moon in my mouth
and letting it go, darting with fishes
in two directions, following their drift.
So slowly, wake me slowly.
Do not stir the water yet.

I suspect my friends of being energetic
They iron shirts before breakfast,
arrive at work on time, leaving
lines of washing hanging out to dry
and supper in the slow cooker.

But I am not an early morning person.
Every morning I collide with time.
Refuse to believe the luminous numerals,
the flashing alarm bell. Too soon
cutting me off from the nibbling fish.

At speed down the by-pass,
I am accused of dream-driving.
I " breathe into this bag madam"
and moon water spills into it and the fishes gasp.

THE DOMESTIC ENGINEER

I'm not just a housewife
let's get things quite clear
around this house here
I'm the domestic engineer.

I deal with dirt.
I'm the dirt expert.
Queen of the machine
I reign supreme
keeping everything clean.
It's a strict routine.

I flick a few switches.
I turn a few knobs.
In a couple of seconds
the whole house throbs.

The dishwasher does the dishes.
The washer cleans the clothes.
The humidi fies, the tumbler dries.
The waste is being disposed.

So please don't call me a housewife.
I'm the domestic engineer.
But if machines go wrong
then a man comes along
to mend them.
I hope that's quite clear.

MY FREEZER

I have something to confess.
My freezer's in a mess.
It's full of food well past its eat by date.
There are lots of little pots.
Their labels have come off.
The contents are a browny sort of grey.

Some pheasants bought when cheap
But how long do they keep?
We were going to have them for a special treat.
There's a plastic box marked 'liver'.
It's been in there forever.
I hardly think it can be fit to eat.

Two burgers in a packet.
A potato in its jacket.
And at the back there's half a Stilton cheese.
Left over cranberry jelly.
Two herrings rather smelly.
And right down at the bottom
there are peas and peas and peas.

ODD SOCKS

What becomes of the odd sock,
the odd sock on the line?
There's always one when you hang them out
but it's not the same one each time.

They all go into the tub in twos
for a gentle woollen wash
but as you count them in and you count them out,
when you hang them out I will hear you shout
"Where's that sock?"

My drawer is full of odd socks.
It's mysterious and weird.
There are long socks and short socks
whose partners have disappeared.

Where are those I carefully chose
to go with clothes; my favourite hose?
Aubergine, that gorgeous hue,
the pair of periwinkle blue.

Bottle green, that certain shade
that shows they're definitely hand made.
There's one of each and that won't do
because with socks, you've got to have two.

So when we meet the next time
please don't make a scene
when you look down at my feet and see
one sock blue, the other, green.

SISTERS 11
(for Jean)

And sometimes
we stay up most of the night
talking. It's a habit
we've dropped into
when I say with her.

We always say
we won't, we'll regret it in the morning
which we do.

It's the best time.
The children are all tucked in.
The men have taken themselves to bed
asking how long we'll be.
Can there be much more to say
after being together all day.
And we tell them 'not long'.

We sit on with our last cup
waiting to talk once more
about warm cake after school
those same suede boots she wore
the sound of her laughter
how our children would have loved her.

AS IF YOU CALL MY NAME

As if you call my name
and I come running,
running to tell you
and you will be resting
in the back room.

And I will come running
holding my sister,
my sister, so young
left too young to fend for herself.
She will climb on your lap
and you will speak echoes,
echoes to comfort in her motherhood.

And I will come running
bringing my lover,
my lover to meet you.
You will notice his hair
darker and stronger
and you will be happy
happy for me your rebellious daughter.

And I will come running
bearing my children,
my children to meet you.
You will see their resemblings
whisper your secrets into their shells.
And your calm will infect them,
infect them for ever.

And I will come running
carrying your man,
your man who mourned
for the rest of his life.
You will hold his frail skull
and you will embrace him,
embrace him until his smiling returns.

And in the back room
you will be resting,
and I will come running,
running to tell you.
As if you call my name.

STARDUST

He said that she was made of stardust
and she sparkled, twinkled
into glittering places, spilling
silver, smiling in her brilliance.

But he meant the big bang
the physics of things. Dust
of the universe. How life began,
the dust to which she will return.

And she is tarnished, dragging
into back alleys. Lacklustre.
A shadow collapsing into blackness.
Leaden ashes in a casket.

IN THE OUTSIDE LANE

You can't help noticing
the fox lying heaped up
in the outside lane,
her fur blooded redder,
white brush showing under.

Cars swerve to avoid her
if they can, but by noon
constant traffic has thrashed
her corpse to tattered fur
helped by crows who dare

to chance their wings
for rich pickings. And soon
only a stain remains
to mark the place, and rain
will wash the stain away.

IN MY ADDRESS BOOK

Your name is still
in my address book
under 'P'.

I imagine writing
quicker to phone
your ghost might still
be there to answer.

To Tipp-Ex out your name
to make space
for another 'P'

would make your death
too permanent for me.

Freda.   10 104.

Julia (Wed)

Suzane   — Links?.

Iris

J.B.J.

Andrew.

Judy (Mike)

(Valerie)

Mary

Dot
(Pam - cream?)

Ruth.